Shine Your Light

Kelli B. Trujillo

wesleyan publishing house
Indianapolis, Indiana

Published by Wesleyan Publishing House
Indianapolis, Indiana 46250
Printed in the United States of America
ISBN: 978-0-89827-561-2
ISBN (e-book): 978-0-89827-811-8

Library of Congress Cataloging-in-Publication Data

Trujillo, Kelli B.
Shine your light / Kelli B. Trujillo.
pages cm. -- (Flourishing faith--devotional studies to fit your life)
Includes bibliographical references.
ISBN 978-0-89827-561-2
1. Christian women--Prayers and devotions. 2. Spiritual life--Christianity--Prayers and devotions. I. Title.
BV4844.T78 2013
242'.643--dc23

2013019573

Visit www.flourishing-faith.com.

Contents

Dedicated in gratitude to the women of Faith Missionary Church in Indianapolis, who are powerfully engaging the world and the local community with the love, grace, and compassion of Jesus.

I'm grateful to my husband David Trujillo. Thank you for insightful discussion and for sharing with me many of the idea-seeds from your teaching that I've explored in this book. I'm also thankful to librarian Laura Burks for helping me acquire all my research materials for this project.

How to Use This Resource

Flourish!

Jesus wants us to have full, abundant, vibrant lives found only through intimate, flourishing faith relationships with him.

But what about when life is so full of demands and responsibilities that we feel too busy to breathe? Is it possible to stay connected with God—to have a flourishing faith—even during the busiest seasons of life? Yes!

Spiritual growth can happen in a variety of ways. And in busy seasons when we can't realistically maintain an hour-long-Bible-study-every-morning habit, we can still connect with God by tuning in to his presence and listening to his voice, moment-by-moment, throughout each day.

Connected

Each day of this thirty-day journey includes three different faith-nourishing experiences in which you can connect with God and deepen your relationship with him. These experiences take just five to fifteen minutes. You can do one in the morning, one midday, and one in the evening. Or you can select just one per day.

Also, you can turn this resource into a ninety-day journey by doing just one experience each day.

Encounter . . . Deepen . . . Grow

Encounter God in a variety of daily experiences:

- **Act:** Apply Scripture's challenges to your life through concrete action.
- **Create:** Use art, drawing, poetry, or another hands-on project to interact with God.
- **Examine:** Explore Scripture using investigation, research, and study.
- **Interact:** Connect with another person as part of your spiritual journey.
- **Internalize:** Interact with Scripture using Christian contemplation, meditation, and memorization.
- **Journal:** Reflect on your journey and record your thoughts in creative ways.
- **Ponder:** Read and think about Scripture, historical information, or an insightful quotation.
- **Pray:** Speak to God and listen to him.
- **Symbolize:** Use an experience or common object as a metaphor to help you contemplate a spiritual truth.
- **Worship:** Express gratitude and praise to God.

Shine Your Light

God calls each of us to be a brilliant, shining light in the world as we proclaim the gospel with our words and deeds. But so often we let fear, negative stereotypes of evangelism, apathy, and insecurity mute our witness and dim our light. And perhaps in the process we lose sight of the powerful good news of God's love at work in our lives.

Refresh your soul by revisiting the good news of Jesus and the gospel's life-changing power in your life. Re-imagine what a gospel-proclaiming life can be! Over the next thirty days, you'll delve into Scripture to engage with the world-changing message of the gospel and hear afresh God's call to share his love and grace with a world in need. You'll invite God to challenge, lead, and empower you to overcome fear and apathy and step boldly into a light-proclaiming life. You'll consider how God is leading you to proclaim the good news through words as well as grace-filled, compassionate action. You'll worship the one who is the Light of the World and also the Light illuminating your life.

Ready your heart. Prepare to meet God. Begin the journey.

Invite others to join you on this journey by downloading a *free* leader's guide for group discussion at **www.flourishing-faith.com.**

days 1–7

Good News!

day 1

Begin

Pray

This is a beginning. The first step onto a path. Where will it lead? Where will you journey with God as your companion? How might you be different—be changed—when you reach the end?

Start by taking in the view—look out at the spiritual vista before you. Ready yourself to press ahead. To encounter. To explore. To discover.

Find a spot to be alone where you can speak aloud to God in prayer. Talk to God about your goals, hopes, and expectations at the start of this spiritual journey. Who are the people you know and love and who you desire to share the light of Christ with? What fears, inadequacies, or questions accompany you on this journey exploring evangelism and outreach? Where are you now, here at the start of this journey, and where do you hope to be by this journey's end?

Journal

Good news! The word *gospel* simply means "good news"; the Greek *euangelion* (from which we derive *evangelism*, *evangelist*, and *evangelical*) also simply means "good news."

But what exactly *is* the "good news"? Grab your journal and jot down some thoughts answering this question. Draw upon your personal story of faith, Scripture passages, or what you most often hear about the "good news" in your church.

Internalize

"Do not be afraid. I bring you good news that will cause great joy for all the people. Today in the town of David a Savior has been born to you; he is the Messiah, the Lord" (Luke 2:10–11).

With these familiar words, an angel, the herald of God, announced to a ragtag group of shepherds that the babe Jesus had been born. We often hear and repeat these words at Christmastime. They carry sentiment, nostalgia, and warm memories of family and carols. But in our familiarity, do we *miss* them? Do we shortchange their power? They are jam-packed with meaning—with life-giving theology and with world-changing truth.

Pause now to prayerfully contemplate what the angel announced and what is revealed to you about the full meaning of the "good news." Phrase by phrase, take in God's Word. Quietly repeat it, think about it, and let each idea nourish you before you move on to the next one.

Do not be afraid.
I bring you good news . . .
. . . great joy for all people . . .
. . . a Savior has been born . . .
. . . he is the Messiah . . .
. . . the Lord.

day 2

God is Love

Examine

"God is love" (1 John 4:16).

Study the following passages that describe God's love. Use your journal to take notes, jotting down key words and phrases and summarizing the main ideas of each passage:

- Deuteronomy 7:7–9
- Nehemiah 9:16–19
- Psalm 36:5–7
- Psalm 86:15
- Psalm 136
- Joel 2:12–13
- Zephaniah 3:17
- Romans 8:37–39
- Ephesians 3:14–19

When you're done, reflect on your notes and consider these questions: Has the idea that "God is love" become a cliché in your life? How can you more fully engage with the powerful reality of God's love?

Ponder

"God's compassion is not something abstract or indefinite, but a concrete, specific gesture in which God reaches out to us," writes Henri Nouwen and his coauthors in their book, *Compassion*. The continue:

> In Jesus Christ we see the fullness of God's compassion. To us, who cry out from the depth of our brokenness

> for a hand that will touch us, an arm that can embrace us, lips that will kiss us, a word that speaks to us here and now, and a heart that is not afraid of our fears and tremblings; to us, who feel our pain as no other human being feels it, has felt it, or ever will feel it and who are always waiting for someone who dares to come close—to us a man has come who could truly say, "I am with you." Jesus Christ, who is God-with-us, has come to us in the freedom of love, not needing to experience our human condition but freely choosing to do so out of love.[1]

How have you experienced longing for the comforting and compassionate love of God? How is your life transformed by the truth that Jesus is with you in this life? How does it affect you when you ponder and focus on God's profound love?

Internalize

John 3:16 is perhaps the most well-known Bible reference in our culture. Displayed at sporting events and memorized by children, this short statement from Jesus' conversation with Nicodemus richly and concisely describes the gospel narrative and the foundational idea that it is all driven by God's profound love.

Spend some time contemplating John 3:16 through the ancient Christian practice of *lectio divina*, Latin for "divine reading" or "sacred reading." It is a way of interacting with Scripture that focuses on prayerful listening with the heart. *Lectio divina* traditionally involves these five steps:

1. Silence (*silencio*): Take a moment to quietly focus on God's presence.

2. Reading (*lectio*): Read the text, slowing down, re-reading, soul-listening.

3. Meditation (*meditato*): Meditate on the text, allowing it to soak in.

4. Prayer (*oratio*): Pray about what you've read.

5. Contemplation (*contemplatio*): Quietly wait on God and focus on his presence.

Deut. 7:7-9 God loves us; He is Faithful

Neh. 9:16-19 God is forgiving, gracious & compassionate, slow to anger & abounding in love.

Psalm 36:5-7 · God is loving, faithful, righteous, just,

" 86:15 compassionate, gracious, slow to anger, loving + faithful

" 136 His love endures forever x 26!

Joel 2:12-13 gracious, compassionate, slow to anger, abounding in love

Zeph. 3:17 He is mighty to save; quiets us, sings over us, rejoices over us w/ singing

Rom 8:37-39 ..... Nothing can separate us from the Love of God.

Eph 3:14-19 .... grasp how wide + long + high and deep is the Love of Christ

day 3

Jesus Loves You

Symbolize

Read 1 John 3:16 and 4:9–10. God's infinite love is expressed to us in many ways, but in no greater manner than the willing sacrifice of Jesus on the cross. The brutal torture and death that Jesus suffered for us is both horrifying and beautiful. The cross itself, a symbol of shame and execution, is now the ultimate symbol of grace, liberty, renewal, and love.

Find some items from nature, and use yarn or string to fashion a simple cross. For example, you could use twigs, dried grasses, wildflowers, or straw to make the crossbeams and wrap twine around them where they intersect to hold it all together.

Hang your cross in a window or set it on your nightstand to serve as a reminder throughout this journey of the profound love Jesus has shown you through his sacrifice.

Internalize

The good news for humankind is also the good news for you. It is a soul-changing truth that you personally experience when you put your faith in Jesus Christ.

The following passages are often used in evangelism. Read them in order, and as you do, intentionally focus on their ramifications in your life. Beyond something you experienced at one time, what ongoing meaning do they have for you now?

- Romans 3:23 all have sinned
- Romans 6:23 wages of sin is death But the gift of God is eter. life
- Romans 5:8 while we were sinners Christ died for us
- Romans 5:1 justified through faith → peace & grace
- Ephesians 2:4–5 saved by Grace because of His love & mercy

Select one of these passages to record in your journal, but personalize it. For example, "But because of his great love for *me* . . ." Let the reality sink in: *You* are saved, forgiven, redeemed, and brought to new and true life through the death and resurrection of Jesus Christ!

Worship

It can become so easy to take Jesus' sacrifice for granted, to treat casually the profound act of love that bought our salvation. Take time now to read or sing all the stanzas of this hymn by Isaac Watts. As you do, join the hymn writer in imagining Jesus' suffering. Offer your heart, your life, your all to Jesus once more.

When I survey the wondrous cross
On which the Prince of glory died,
My richest gain I count but loss,
And pour contempt on all my pride.

Forbid it, Lord, that I should boast,
Save in the death of Christ my God!
All the vain things that charm me most,
I sacrifice them to his blood.

See from his head, his hands, his feet,
Sorrow and love flow mingled down!
Did e'er such love and sorrow meet,
Or thorns compose so rich a crown?

Were the whole realm of nature mine,
That were a present far too small;
Love so amazing, so divine,
Demands my soul, my life, my all.

To Christ, who won for sinners grace
By bitter grief and anguish sore,
Be praise from all the ransomed race
Forever and forevermore.[2]

Rom. 5:1 Because I (Donna) have been justified through (my personal act of) faith (in Jesus as the Son of God) I have peace with God through our Lord Jesus Christ, through whom I (Donna) have gained access by faith into this grace in which I now stand.

day 4

Love Redefined

Ponder

God loves you personally.

But it is critical to understand that the love of God is much more than simply a personal love for us as individuals. God's expansive love for all of humanity certainly *does* involve inviting us into a personal relationship with him, but God's love is much, much more.

As we grow to understand more of who God is, our meager and limited human understanding of love is shattered. In its place, we discover a love that is robust, vibrant, and expansive.

In Scripture we discover a God who values justice; who is enraged when the poor and outcast are trampled upon. And we discover a God who welcomes—a God who taught his people to care for aliens and immigrants, provide for outcasts, and include the lonely.

Read Deuteronomy 10:17–19; Isaiah 58; Amos 5:10–15, 21–24; and Zechariah 7:8–10. These are not lovey-dovey passages. In fact, they contain serious warnings and even anger! But they reveal who God is and what he values. They help us discover a bit more about what God's love really means.

Create

"Sometimes we are tempted to reduce the gospel to individuals being reconciled to God personally or even to

God forming our own special community," says Scot McKnight. "But . . . God's work is *with* the whole world and *for* the whole world. . . . God's loving arms are around the globe, around adults and trees and mountains, children and rivers and birds, moms and dads and lions and elephants, little poor children and adult poor people and cultures and ethnicities, and governments and art shows and building projects. Around golf courses and sweat shops, around country clubs and inner-city slums, around high-rise penthouses and humans in ghettos."[3]

What does it mean to proclaim "For God so loved the world" (John 3:16)? Who is encompassed in God's generous embrace? What does this big, compassionate, merciful, just, and welcoming love look like?

Grab some scissors and glue, then use your local newspaper, magazines, junk mail, and old photos to create a simple collage that represents God's expansive, robust love. Select images of faces, photos from current events, and words from the headlines that can represent the world God profoundly loves. Let your collage serve to remind you of God's love and challenge you keep your view of God's love from becoming sentimental and small.

Interact

Use social media (or a phone call or personal interaction) to ask several friends: What does it mean to you that "God is love" (1 John 4:8) and that "God so loved the world" (John 3:16)? Why does God's love matter, and what does it mean?

What insights do your friends' answers give you about God's love and about how we often think about God's love?

How do their answers compare or contrast with some of the Old Testament teachings that reveal how God's love is infused with justice, compassion, mercy, and welcome? How many friends focused on their personal relationship with God? How many emphasized God's global love and concern for all people?

day 5

Jesus' Good News

Internalize

Read Luke 4:14–22.

Jesus identified himself as the fulfillment of the Old Testament prophesies and teachings about God's justice, compassion, and welcome. Quoting from Isaiah 58:6 and 61:1–2, Jesus launched his ministry by proclaiming this as his mission. Immediately following his baptism and temptation in the wilderness, Jesus boldly declared that this is what he's all about. According to Jesus, God's concern for justice and his compassionate love for the vulnerable are essential to our understanding of the "good news."

Reread what Jesus said and mull over it. How often do you hear these kinds of ideas reflected in the way people normally talk about the gospel? Have we lost sight of a critical component of Jesus' teaching and proclamation? Do we really understand how central these values of compassion and justice are to the good news?

Create

Within the church, we have various visual methods of communicating the gospel. Children, for example, are taught the "wordless book"—a series of colored paper or beads that symbolize scriptural truths. (Green: God created the world; black: our hearts are darkened by sin; and so on.) Another common visual representation of the gospel is a simple sketch of a stick figure standing at the end of a large chasm. (The chasm is sin, and it separates the person from God; no matter how far the figure jumps or how "good" he or she is, reaching the other side is impossible without God. Only he can bridge the chasm with the cross.)

Jesus' presentation of the gospel in Luke 4:14–22 is also rich with imagery; phrase by phrase, we can picture these scenes of liberation and restoration in our minds.

In your journal, sketch some images or symbols that capture the ideas Jesus proclaimed he was all about. (For example, you could sketch shackles that are open or unlocked.) Imagine how these visual images provide insight into the full meaning of the gospel for individuals and humankind.

Journal

"Most of us know that Jesus suffered and died to set us free from the power of sin, but that is only part of the gospel story. His mission and message actually extend far beyond that," says author Julie Clawson. "By setting people free from the oppression of sin within us, Jesus enables us to live differently from the oppressive and unjust systems of the world around us as well. His life, death and resurrection inaugurated a new kingdom, and he taught his disciples to live according to the revolutionary values of this kingdom of God: to care for the needy, to treat one's enemies with love, to feed the hungry, to work for justice."[4]

In your journal, reflect on this quote. How do Clawson's ideas compare or contrast with the way the gospel has been presented and explained to you? What's your reaction to this larger understanding of the gospel story and Jesus' mission? How do these ideas challenge you?

day 6

The King and His Kingdom

Journal

"Jesus went throughout Galilee, teaching in their synagogues, proclaiming *the good news of the kingdom*, and healing every disease and sickness among the people" (Matt. 4:23, emphasis added; see also Mark 1:14–15; Luke 4:43).

For Jesus, the good news and the kingdom are interwoven and inseparable. In essence, Jesus' teachings about his kingdom *are* his teachings about the gospel—about his rule as Lord in our lives today, about the values of his reign, about his future victory and ultimate restoration of all things, about the life-transforming treasure of salvation that is worth everything to us.

The gospel of the kingdom isn't only about God's future reign over all things; it is also about Jesus' reign of compassion, justice, liberty, grace, and restoration in our lives right now.

In your journal, reflect on these ideas. How do you feel personally challenged or inspired by Jesus' linking of the gospel and the kingdom? How might you need to reorient your perspective on the gospel—what it is, what it means to share it, what it means to live within it—in light of Jesus' emphasis on this kingdom and its values?

Pray

The kingdom of God is not only a future reality, but also a present one. When Jesus lived on earth, he announced its fulfillment and presence—even though its culmination had not yet (and has not yet) occurred. It is an already-but-not-yet reality.[5]

Consider how different English translations communicate what Jesus said about his kingdom:

- "From that time on, Jesus began to preach, 'Repent, for the kingdom of heaven has come near'" (Matt. 4:17).
- ". . . is at hand" (Matt. 4:17 ESV).
- ". . . is near" (Matt. 4:17 NLT).
- "The kingdom of God is in your midst" (Luke 17:21).
- ". . . is in the midst of you" (Luke 17:21 ESV).
- ". . . is already among you" (Luke 17:21 NLT).

Prayerfully reread these passages. Invite God to help you dwell on the immediacy and current reality of the kingdom and on the miraculous presence of its King, Jesus.

Turn these passages into a simple prayer. Or, if you'd like, use these words:

Jesus you came near to them as you come near to me.
Help me to grasp the at-hand reality of your kingdom.
Be my king. Form my life by your kingdom values.
King Jesus, you are near. You are at hand. You are with me now. Amen.

Worship

Focus your heart on the reality that the kingdom of God will ultimately rule in this world someday. Worship God by speaking or singing the hymn "Jesus Shall Reign."

Jesus shall reign where'er the sun
Does his successive journeys run;
His kingdom stretch from shore to shore,
Till moons shall wax and wane no more.

People and realms of every tongue
Dwell on his love with sweetest song;
And infant voices shall proclaim
Their early blessings on his name.

Blessings abound where'er he reigns;
The prisoner leaps to lose his chains;
The weary find eternal rest,
And all the sons of want are blessed.

Let every creature rise and bring
[Their special] honors to our King;
Angels descend with songs again,
And earth repeat the loud amen![6]

day 7

Jesus is the Light

Worship

Among the many biblical motifs that surround and describe Jesus, one of the most beautiful and profound is the idea of light. Light frees us from darkness, enables us to see, reveals color and beauty, warms us, and causes growth.

Jesus, as the ancient Nicene Creed declared, is "Light of Light, very God of very God."[7] Jesus is the illumination for all, the true hope of life.

Read these passages from the gospel of John: 1:5, 9; 8:12; 9:5; 12:35–36, 46. What do they reveal about Jesus? What impression do they give of his mission? How do they speak to you personally about what Jesus has brought and is bringing to your life?

Let your pondering lead you into worship. Speak words of gratitude and praise aloud to God.

Journal

Quietly ponder the words of this old Russian hymn:

As light, O Christ, Thou cam'st to earth;
In Thee I live, in Thee I shall arise;
Thou art my joy, Thou my new birth,
To blessed life Thou openest mine eyes.
For me Thou to the cross didst go,
For me Thou gav'st Thy blood to flow.

For me, in dark Gethsemane
Alone Thou, Christ, with sin and death didst fight;
Alone with God didst plead for me,
That I in Thee might see the blessed light.
From all my heart, while I may live,
Eternal thanks to Thee I'll give.[8]

In your journal, reflect on these questions: How is Jesus a light to me? How is the gospel good news to me? How has the good news of Jesus' loving sacrificed enlightened my life?

Create

Decorate a clear glass votive candleholder. Then set a votive or tea light candle inside and let it symbolize the truth that Jesus is the Light. Try one of these easy ideas:

- Cut various colors of tissue paper into shapes and use diluted glue to layer them in a collage on the exterior of the candleholder to look like stained glass.
- Use fabric scraps and diluted glue to make an opaque collage.
- Cut contact paper into simple shapes and affix them to the outside of the candleholder.
- Write words (like *Jesus* or *Light*) or draw images on clear contact paper, then affix it to the outside of the candleholder.

Have fun! And whenever you light your candle, take a moment to tune your heart to the truth: Jesus is the Light of the World!

days 8–14

Good-News Words

day 8

Called to Be Light

Create

Jesus the Light said, "You are the light of the world. A town built on a hill cannot be hidden. Neither do people light a lamp and put it under a bowl. Instead they put it on its stand, and it gives light to everyone in the house. In the same way, let your light shine before others, that they may see your good deeds and glorify your Father in heaven" (Matt. 5:14–16).

You are called by the Light to be light.

In your journal, write some poetry, playing with the idea of light. Explore things like the light of salvation, what Jesus' light is like, what it means to be called a light, how light shines in your personal darkness, or anything else that comes to mind. Have fun creatively expressing feelings, images, or ideas that speak to your soul.

Ponder

Jesus calls us, his followers, to be "the light of the world" (Matt. 5:14). Just as he invited his first disciples, he invites us to follow him (Matt. 4:19). Like he instructed his disciples, he tasks us with proclaiming his kingdom (Matt. 10:7). He commissions us to make disciples (Matt. 28:19). He charges us to be his witnesses (Acts 1:8).

Receiving the good news means entering into a light way of life. It's a new way of being: a way of shining, following, kingdom-proclaiming, disciple-making, and witnessing to Jesus' words, deeds, and identity.

This is not an optional part of Christianity, and it's not meant to be something we have to plan for or work up the gumption to say or something to feel incessantly guilty about not doing enough of. Instead, by the very nature of the Light within you, you're called to shine.

In prayerful honesty and in awareness of God's unfailing grace, consider these questions: Are you living a life that follows Jesus? Are you dedicated to proclaiming God's kingdom? How are you making disciples? Are you a trusted and accurate witness? Do you live as a light? How well do you really understand your light-identity as a Christian?

Symbolize

"Do everything without grumbling or arguing, so that you may become blameless and pure, 'children of God without fault in a warped and crooked generation.' Then you will shine among them like stars in the sky as you hold firmly to the word of life" (Phil. 2:14–16).

You are made by God and placed right where you are to be a shining and brilliant light, like a luminous star in a dark sky.

Wait until it gets dark, then sit outside and stargaze. Notice the nearest and brightest stars. See if you can recognize constellations. Look intently for the glimmer of distant stars whose pale light may be harder to see. Invite God to help you understand more deeply what it means for you to shine like a star in the universe.

day 9

The E-Word

interact

Evangelism can be a big, scary word. It can be loaded with guilt ("I'm not doing enough!"), insecurity ("I don't have the right gifts or personality!"), and intimidation ("I don't know what to say or how to answer questions!"). It can also carry with it negative stereotypes: obnoxious street preachers droning on about hell, cult-like door-to-door distributors of tracts, overly polished TV personalities asking for more funds while saving souls, and aggressive apologists ready to humiliate any atheist who dares enter the ring with them.

Along with these impressions is the common idea that evangelism must be done a certain way, such as an elaborate outline of memorized Bible passages, a series of questions about the afterlife, a tract about God's laws, an in-depth discussion of heady apologetics arguments, and so on.

So what is evangelism, really?

Use social media, the phone, or in-person conversations to invite your Christian friends to respond briefly to these three questions:

1. What is evangelism? Define it.
2. What should it look like?
3. Why is evangelism important?

How do your friends' answers freshen your perspective as you begin to think more deeply about your personal call to share the good news with others?

Ponder

"Preach the gospel at all times. If necessary, use words."[1] There is profound truth in this statement in the sense that one's life—actions and demeanor—absolutely *do* "preach" a message.

But there can also be a false assumption we make when we mistakenly take this idea too far: the notion that using words is often unnecessary. The idea that a life lived well is enough—that somehow the gospel will effuse from our lives without a word being said. This simply is not what Jesus asked of his first followers, or of us.

Words are necessary.

They were essential in Jesus' ministry: "Jesus went throughout Galilee, teaching in their synagogues, *proclaiming the good news of the kingdom*" (Matt. 4:23, emphasis added). And he sent his disciples out to do the very same thing: "As you go, *proclaim* this message: 'The kingdom of heaven has come near'" (Matt. 10:7, emphasis added).

The good news of the kingdom, God's love, Jesus' saving sacrifice—these life-changing truths are communicated in words and are in the Word of God and in our words to others.

When were good-news words initially spoken to you? How are they still spoken into your life? How can speaking good-news words to others become a more natural and instinctive part of your life?

internalize

What does evangelism look like?

Use a devotional reading practice developed by Ignatius of Loyola in the 1500s to help you dig deep into John 4:1–42:

- Pray, asking God to guide your thoughts as you mentally step inside the passage, imagining what it was like.
- Read the passage, then use your God-given imagination to picture the scene. What might it have felt, looked, sounded, and smelled like that day near the well? How do you imagine Jesus' tone of voice? How did his words impact the woman? What might it have been like to be there with Jesus? What did she sound and look like as she told others?
- Personally respond to Jesus in prayer.

The woman at the well instinctively responded to her encounter with Jesus by telling others of her experience and inviting them to come see him too. How does this natural response of honest sharing inspire you?

day 10

The Fear Barrier

Symbolize

There are many fears that can stifle our efforts to share the gospel. We may desire to speak God's truth, but we instead keep quiet. We see those in need of Christ's love, but our fears form a barrier that hold us back.

Go and look out a window. See the world outside, then focus on and touch the transparent barrier—the glass—between you and the outside world.

Prayerfully think about the specific fears that hold you back from evangelism. What worries or concerns form a barrier, preventing you from really reaching out to others with good-news words? Think of specific situations in which you held back from talking about God with someone you care about; honestly assess what it was that held you back. Some of your concerns may be quite valid, while others may be fears that you are granting too much power in your life.

Pray about the fears that come to mind:

God, each day you reveal to me a world of people who need your love. I confess that these fears are holding me back: _______________ (name specific fears). *Please shatter the barrier of fear in my life and fill me with the courage to love others with your good-news words. Amen.*

interact

Identify a trusted Christian friend or mentor whose spiritual life inspires you. Contact her and ask her to pray for you as you journey through this exploration of evangelism and outreach. Take courage and name some specific fears or other barriers you feel are holding you back from evangelism. Ask your friend to pray that God will help you find the power and courage to overcome those specific fears as you grow in your understanding and practice of evangelism.

journal

Read John 20:11–18. In this passage, Mary Magdalene was the first of Jesus' followers to see the risen Christ. Explore this passage and take note of her response.

Mary Magdalene became a bold proclaimer. She declared to the others, "I have seen the Lord!" (v. 18). Emboldened by her personal encounter with Jesus, she confidently and courageously announced the reality that changed everything for her (and for all the world).

Reflect in your journal. It is important to honestly acknowledge fears related to evangelism—fears that are a reality for all of us. But even in light of those fears, can you be a bold proclaimer like Mary? Answer these questions: What does it mean for you to boldly live an "I have seen the Lord!" life? What fears must you overcome? How are you inspired by Mary's bold proclamation?

day 11

How *Not* to Witness

Create

Have you ever cringed when you've observed a Christian evangelizing in an obnoxious or embarrassing way? Or have you ever noticed stereotypical depictions of Christians (on TV or movies) who are witnessing, but are completely nerdy, stupid, strange, prudish, or in some other way humiliating and repellant?

Think through some examples of bad evangelism you've encountered in your life, church, or the culture at large. Also consider how non-Christians perceive or stereotype Christian evangelism. Now grab a pen and sketch some silly caricatures of these various perceptions, exaggerating what seems bad or unappealing about each stereotype. You could even give your caricatures silly names or fill speech bubbles with the types of things each person might say.

These cringe-inducing examples and stereotypes can become one of the biggest barriers to evangelism for many of us; we strongly desire to differentiate ourselves from "those Christians": the in-your-face know-it-alls; the seemingly unthinking, blind followers; the sheltered, uncultured weirdos; and the Christians who simply come off as great big jerks! We don't want our friends to think we're like them, so we keep quiet.

But the reality is that we can be bold without being obnoxious, and we can be confident without being a know-it-all!

Though this exercise is lighthearted, use it to help you honestly evaluate how you *don't* want to approach evangelism . . . and how you *do.*

Examine

None of us is perfect. We all have faults and failings! But Scripture is pretty clear that we're to embody a Christlike demeanor in our interactions with others. This is especially true in evangelism!

Read and take notes on the following passages describing how we can honor God in the way we speak with and listen to others: Proverbs 15:28; 16:24; 17:27; 18:1, 12–13.

Now read and take notes on these passages describing a God-honoring demeanor: Galatians 5:22–23 and Philippians 2:1–16.

When considered all together, what portrait do these passages paint of how a Christian ought to interact with others? How can a Christian witness from a posture of kindness, empathy, and authentic listening? Why is a believer's demeanor toward others such an essential component of evangelism?

Pray

Review the passages listed above. Which verse particularly stands out to you, challenging you in an area of needed growth in your character or demeanor toward others? Memorize it by repeating it several times to yourself, then pray, asking God to help you grow in this area, especially when it comes to your interactions with non-Christians.

day 12

Lost and Found

Examine

Living as a shining light means sharing good-news words. And rather than brash or obnoxious caricatures of evangelism, we truly shine when we learn how and what to proclaim from the Master.

Consider these stories Jesus used to communicate the good news to a group of tax collectors and sinners in Luke 15: the parable of the lost sheep (vv. 1–7), the parable of the lost coin (vv. 8–10), and the parable of the lost son (vv. 11–32). Read each parable, pausing to reflect and take notes on these questions after each one: What is Jesus communicating about humanity in this story? What does this parable emphasize about God? How would you summarize the main message of this parable in a sentence?

When you're done, review your notes. How are these truths about humanity, God, and salvation personally meaningful to you? How might they be life-changing for a non-Christian you know?

Symbolize

Dig through your purse to find a coin; then hold it in your hand. As you hold it, read Luke 15:8–10 aloud.

Part of what Jesus was communicating in this parable is a profound message about God's love: like the lost coin for which a woman intensely searched, you matter.

Look at the coin, turn it over in your hand, and squeeze it tight. How can this small story in Scripture help you understand, more deeply, how God feels about you? And, ultimately, how can Jesus' story enable you to see how God feels about the non-Christians in your life?

You are loved by God. You are significant to God. You matter.

Have they heard this message? Do they need to hear it? What difference might this message make in an unbeliever's life—in his or her sense of identity and purpose?

Pray and ask God to help the meaning of this parable sink into your heart as you consider your role in sharing good-news words with others.

Journal

In Luke 15, Jesus told three parables that repeat a similar theme. It is a message of a God who loves the lost. It is a message that says each person is significant to God. It communicates that God will go (and did go!) to great lengths to rescue the lost. It emphasizes how that rescue—that finding and repentance—is a great joy to God. It reveals that God is the ultimate loving Father who utterly forgives and exuberantly welcomes, no matter what. These are truths people hunger and thirst for!

Consider these thoughts from Brennan Manning: "Healing becomes the opportunity to pass off to another human being what I have received from the Lord Jesus; namely His unconditional acceptance of me as I am, not as I should be. He loves me whether in a state of grace or disgrace, whether I live up to the lofty expectations of His gospel or I don't. He comes to me where I live and loves me as I am."[2]

Revisit Luke 15:11–32, then reflect in your journal:

- How have you been healed, welcomed, and accepted by God?
- How does Manning's angle on "healing"—sharing God's acceptance, grace, and welcome with others—inspire you as you think about evangelism?

day 13

Real Life

Ponder

We often talk about having a relationship with Jesus. But who *is* this Jesus? As we understand more of what he said about himself, we enter into a greater understanding of the gospel.

Jesus spoke many crucial statements about himself that make clear that he is the Messiah (Mark 14:61–62), the Son of God (John 10:22–39), and the only way to the Father (John 14:6). But let's focus now on some powerful metaphors Jesus used to describe himself in the gospel of John:

- the bread of life (6:48–51),
- the living water (4:10–14; 7:37–38),
- the light of the world (8:12; 9:5), and
- the resurrection and the life (11:25).

These word pictures provide a powerful insight. The gospel is not only about being saved from sin and death, but also about being ushered into true soul satisfaction. It is a life-transforming reality: a relationship with the Bread that truly nourishes, the Light that allows us to really see, the Water that quenches our soul's deepest thirsts, the real Life we were meant to live.

These metaphors speak profoundly to the deep longings and yearnings within every human soul. How do you experience satisfaction and nourishment in Jesus? How does Jesus' message about himself speak to the longing in the lives of non-Christians you know and care about?

Symbolize

Drink something refreshing. Eat something satisfying. And if you're able, sit outside in the sun and soak in the light.

As you do, pray and think about your Savior who is the Bread of Life (John 6:48–51), the Living Water (John 4:10–14), and the Light of the World (John 8:12). Consider the soul-nourishment that Jesus brings to your life and that he offers to each of us. Jesus said, "I have come that they may have life, and have it to the full" (John 10:10). Thank God for bringing satisfaction to your deepest needs—a satisfaction you experience in part now, but will fully experience in heaven with God.

Journal

Think about some of the non-Christians in your life: people you live near or work with: friends, family members, colleagues, and acquaintances. Write some of their names in your journal, and then try to empathize with their experience of life without Christ. Use these prompts to guide your writing:

- What parts of this person's life might be "dark"—a sense of hopelessness, confusion, discouragement, loneliness, or guilt?
- What are some of the deepest longings in this person's life?
- What does he or she ultimately hunger and thirst for?
- How are these longings apparent in feelings, choices, and general human experiences?

When we come to know Jesus and follow him, we certainly don't have all of our problems solved, negative emotions wiped away, and longings erased! But we *do* find in him a robust hope that can sustain us through painful or confusing times, and we find a sense of identity, purpose, and joy in a relationship with Christ that fulfills us.

How does this empathy exercise help as you consider how to share good-news words with your friends or loved ones? How might you share the idea that Jesus is the light we all need and the satisfaction we all long for?

day 14

Appealing . . . but incomplete?

Ponder

In an effort to make their message appealing, Christians sometimes inadvertently present a gospel that is dangerously incomplete. An incomplete gospel emphasizes one key idea to the detriment of others. While true, it is missing some absolutely essential ideas. It's appealing, but it can end up being dangerous because it is only partly true. It can lead to distorted disciples with an off-kilter walk. And when it ends up not jiving with a person's actual experience or with Scripture's teachings, it can lead to confusion, disappointment, and even altogether abandonment of Christianity.

For example:

- "You can spend eternity in heaven (rather than hell) after you die!" True! But a gospel proclamation focused so much on the afterlife skips over a huge part of Jesus' teaching about the here and now. Being saved isn't just about where a person ends up; it has significant implications for one's identity, spiritual journey, and purpose on earth today.
- "God has a wonderful plan for your life!" True! But Jesus also assured us that his followers would have trouble in this life (John 16:33). Following Jesus *is* wonderful, but it also requires a lot: pain, struggle, sacrifice, obedience, and death to self (Luke 9:23).

- "You can have a personal relationship with Jesus!" True! But the New Testament says very little about a personal relationship and it says a lot about the church and the kingdom. The gospel is personal, but it is not individualistic. It is an invitation into something much bigger than yourself.

Think about this issue for a moment: Do you agree that an incomplete gospel is dangerous? What other incomplete gospel proclamations have you heard? How can these skewed messages lead to trouble?

Symbolize

Prepare a favorite food—something simple (like homemade popcorn or trail mix) or something more elaborate (grandma's muffin recipe or homemade pasta sauce).

If you were to leave out an ingredient, how would it affect the final product? How would popcorn taste without a sprinkling of salt? What about muffins without flour or pasta sauce without olive oil?

Which ingredients are essential and which are not? In terms of evangelism, what are the essential elements of the gospel? What truths or ideas are most important to discuss with a spiritually curious friend? What other ideas are less essential and can be set aside for later discussions?

Interact

In *Humanitarian Jesus*, Ron Sider says,

> A lot of evangelicalism thinks the gospel is forgiveness of sins. What really matters is that your sins are forgiven

> so that you can go to heaven when you die. I want to say that's flatly unbiblical. It's not because it's untrue. It's a crucial part of the gospel, but for Jesus, the gospel is the good news of the kingdom. . . . So when I talk about evangelism, I mean inviting people who are not now Christians to accept Jesus Christ as their personal Lord and Savior and to accept his gospel. But that gospel is not just the forgiveness of sins so you can go to heaven; it is also the good news that his kingdom is breaking in.[3]

Use social networking or e-mail to share this quote along with Matthew 10:7 with friends. Ask them: What's your reaction to this quote, and what do you think it looks like to proclaim the good news of the kingdom?

Springboard off their responses to more deeply explore Sider's ideas for yourself. How can a gospel proclamation focused entirely on personal salvation be incomplete? How can your good-news words more adequately reflect Jesus' teachings about the good news of the kingdom?

days 15–21

Good–News Actions

day 15

Lives That Proclaim

Ponder

There's a way you can speak more eloquently than the most learned sermon, more beautifully than the most artistic poem and more persuasively than the most polished speech. You can speak with your life. Your actions, demeanor, choices, way of being—together these proclaim a message to the world.

Consider Peter's challenge: "Live such good lives among the pagans that . . . they may see your good deeds and glorify God on the day he visits us" (1 Pet. 2:12). This is evangelism—good-news actions proclaiming the gospel that lead to transformed lives.

Our lives proclaim the gospel as we embody the values of God. As people see in us a glimpse of God's transcendent truth, grace-filled kingdom, and unconditional love, the good news for all humankind is powerfully proclaimed.

How can a person's life evangelize? What is it that people thirst for, and how can Christians embody God's answer? What glimpses of God and his truth do others long to see and experience? How does your life proclaim the good news?

Journal

In *The Colors of Hope*, author Richard Dahlstrom says,

I'm called to more, much more, than simply surviving, protecting my assets and reputation while, as a footnote,

I drop a little money in the offering and tell my neighbors Jesus died for them. Such a small view of God's activity in my life, and God's calling on my days, is part of the reason so many find Christianity boring. But let's not confuse this caricature of the Christian life with the real thing. . . . Trusting in God's active involvement in our daily lives, we're invited to learn dependence on the Creator for provision, direction, and protection. Then, from this place of security, we're invited to live outwardly, finding creative ways to spill hope into the world.[1]

Open your journal. At the top of one page, write "A Small View" and at the top of another write "A Hope-Spilling Life." Reflect on Dahlstrom's quote and take notes on each page. When have you observed a small view of following Jesus or a caricature of Christianity? And what could a secure, outward-looking, hope-spilling way of life look like? Describe examples, character traits, attitudes, and actions of each mind-set. Reflect honestly on where you see each of these perspectives in your habits and way of life.

Pray

Dedicate this day to a gospel-proclaiming way of being, and invite God to help you. Several times today (perhaps once every hour), check in with God and pray a simple prayer based on 1 Peter 2:12. Use something like this:

Today, help me, God, to live a life that draws others to glorify you. Amen.

day 16

A "Light" Way of Life

Examine

"You are the light of the world," Jesus said. "Let your light shine before others, that they may see your good deeds and glorify your Father in heaven" (Matt. 5:14, 16).

How can one live a life that shines the light of Christ?

This passage, recorded in Matthew 5, is near the beginning of Jesus' Sermon on the Mount—a powerful portrait of kingdom living, describing in detail many of the counterculture values and choices that are to characterize a follower of Christ. Jesus began the sermon by telling us that our lives are to shine the good news (Matt. 5:14–16), and then he explains how that ought to happen.

Read Jesus' entire Sermon on the Mount in Matthew 5–7. Select one of these note-taking methods to guide your study:

- List all of the main topics Jesus discussed. Then in one sentence or less, try to summarize Jesus' key teaching on each topic.
- Read the entire passage, reflect on it, then create a list of ten to twenty adjectives or phrases that describe what a person living according to Jesus' teachings is like.
- If your Bible has headings that divide the passage, ignore them. Take notes on how you'd group the verses and passages, then create headings that touch on the key teachings in each section.

When you're done studying the passage, aim to keep thinking about it throughout the day, asking God, "How can my life shine more brightly to the world around me?"

Internalize

Jesus' Sermon on the Mount, describing the ethics of his kingdom, convicts us to the core. Over and over we see what a light-way-of-life looks like and how glaringly contrary it is to our instincts, selfishness, and pride. Skim the sermon in Matthew 5–7, and select one verse or paragraph that is particularly convicting to you.

Record the passage in your journal, then spend time memorizing it. As you repeat it to yourself, let its meaning sink in. Prayerfully consider how God is challenging you to embody good-news actions—to live a light way of life.

Create

Reflect on Matthew 5:14–16. What does it mean to be a light? To live in a way that shines? What images or ideas does this metaphor bring to mind for you?

Grab some paper and write a free-verse poem exploring the idea of a light way of life. Springboard off of ideas and word pictures in Jesus' Sermon on the Mount in Matthew 5–7. Write creatively and expressively—have fun! Let Jesus' words inspire you and simply respond.

day 17

A Servant's Life

Internalize

With an awareness of God's presence and an attitude of prayerful listening, engage your imagination as you read John 13:1–17. Try to picture the scene—visualize the details, imagine the sounds one might hear during the meal, consider what each spoken word might have sounded like. Imagine Jesus' and the disciples' faces and body language. Step inside the account.

As you allow the scene to come to life in your mind, prayerfully think through these questions:

- What is so compelling about Jesus' actions?
- What do you think Peter felt and thought by the end of this encounter?
- How do Jesus' words and example speak to you personally? Why?
- How do you sense the Holy Spirit prompting you to respond?

Journal

One of the most significant good-news actions a person can do is one that can be hard to see. It's often behind the scenes, away from the spotlight, performed without fanfare or attention. It's service.

Jesus, the King of Kings and Lord of Lords, took on the humble and humiliating role of foot-washer, cleansing his disciples' feet of dust, debris, and likely even dung from their journey along first-century streets. It was a task reserved for servants and slaves. Yet Jesus did it, and he said, "I have set you an example that you should do as I have done for you" (John 13:15).

If we follow Jesus, we do as he has done: We serve. We willingly take on lowly tasks and humbling roles. We live a gospel that says the self comes last rather than first. We heed Paul's urging: "Do nothing out of selfish ambition or vain conceit. Rather, in humility value others above yourselves, not looking to your own interests but each of you to the interests of others. In your relationships with one another, have the same mind-set as Christ Jesus" (Phil. 2:3–5). In his humble, servant-attitude, we reveal a bit of Jesus to the world.

Reflect on these ideas in your journal. How can a life of humble service proclaim the good news? What internal struggles or external realities make it difficult for you to serve others? To have Jesus' mind-set of humility?

Act

Do something to serve others. Yes, it's that simple.

Service is probably part of your day already. You can transform a normal, menial task into a spiritually meaningful act of service simply by focusing on Christ, honoring him in your act, and fostering an attitude of humility and love for others as you perform it.

Doing the laundry, loading the dishwasher, prepping dinner—service. Listening to a coworker, completing a job with excellence, showing courtesy to a customer—service. Changing a diaper, wiping a runny nose, helping with homework—service. Whatever your daily routine, opportunities abound to serve in the same humble mind-set that Jesus exemplified for us (John 13:1–17; Phil. 2:5).

You live the good news as you serve.

day 18

A Just Life

Examine

Scripture repeatedly emphasizes that God cares about the outcast, the vulnerable, the abused, and the overlooked. Our lives shine with God's character when we live as people of compassion and justice.

Read the following passages that are just a sampling of the Bible's teachings on justice:

- Proverbs 31:8–9
- Isaiah 1:11–17
- Isaiah 58:1–14
- Isaiah 61:1–3, 8
- Jeremiah 22:3
- Amos 5:10–15, 21–24
- Micah 6:8
- Zechariah 7:9–10

Take notes using these questions: How would you summarize the main idea of these passages in your words? Based on the context, how is justice understood in these passages? What does biblical justice mean? What is it to look like?

Ponder

"When I preach, I have just one text to preach from, and I always preach from this one. My text is 'When I Found Jesus,'" explained Sojourner Truth.[2] But the text of Sojourner Truth's *life* was far beyond simply sharing her personal testimony. Raised in slavery, she escaped to freedom when she was twenty-nine years old. Eventually, Truth began powerfully speaking out against the injustice of slavery. She worked actively as an abolitionist until she died at the age of eighty-six.

As a young woman, Amy Carmichael sensed the call to mission work and eventually moved to India. There she met a very young little girl who'd been sold into forced prostitution as part of the local "worship" practices at the temple. Carmichael sheltered and cared for the girl rather than return her to a life of sexual abuse. Despite the threat of criminal prosecution, Carmichael began a ministry which eventually saved thousands of children from forced temple prostitution.[3]

Dorothy Day lived a "wild" life; she was friends with radical socialists, jailed for protesting for women's suffrage, and underwent an illegal abortion. But eventually Day was drawn to Jesus, and her life began to dramatically change. Day sought to take Christ's teachings about caring for the poor literally. Soon her home became a shelter for the homeless and destitute, and she lived among them. Over time, Day founded dozens of similar homes for the poor.[4]

From different times, different cultures, and vastly different experiences, Sojourner Truth, Amy Carmichael, and Dorothy Day all reveal a powerful lesson: Proclaiming the gospel is not only about a personal faith. The gospel is proclaimed through a life of justice and concern for the poor and vulnerable. God used these women to change lives. How can God use you?

Act

In Acts 6:1–7, the early church tasked Stephen and six others with a critical job: ensuring that the needs of the widows in their community were met. Right from the beginning, concern for the poor and vulnerable was an essential value of the church. This same concern continues to motivate us today: God calls us, right where we live, to be people who "act justly and to love mercy and to walk humbly with [our] God" (Mic. 6:8).

What are the needs in your community? Where are the poor, the vulnerable, the outcast, and the overlooked? How is God using Christians to wade into these areas of need and live out God's justice and mercy?

Research specific needs and ministries in your local community. Contact someone in your church to learn more about what they're doing, or use the Internet to gather information about local ministry organizations. As you research, pray about what you learn and ask God to clearly guide you if he wants you to get involved.

day 19

A Welcoming Life

Ponder

"Share with the Lord's people who are in need. Practice hospitality" (Rom. 12:13).

Hospitality. It is a word we often associate with well-prepared tables and nicely cooked meals, the nourishment and blessing of food and comfort. In fact, Jesus himself used the idea of a banquet to teach about hospitality.

Read Luke 14:12–14. In this passage, says theologian Christine Pohl, "Jesus challenges narrow definitions and dimensions of hospitality and presses them outward to include those with whom one least desires to have connections. The poor and infirm come with their inconvenient needs and condition, with their incapacity to reciprocate. But in welcoming them one anticipates and reflects the welcome of God."[5]

Immediately after this teaching on hospitality, Jesus told a parable about the kingdom of God (Luke 14:15–24). In this parable, it is again the poor, crippled, blind, and lame who come to enjoy the great heavenly banquet. The hospitality Jesus asked his followers to exhibit is paralleled in the heavenly hospitality of God.

Growing up out of a heart that has been generously and graciously welcomed by God, followers of Jesus are to respond by offering God's welcome to others. A welcome that says, "You are not excluded here. You are not too poor or too dirty or too sinful or too ugly or too different. No accomplishments or accoutrements required. You are welcome at this table. You are welcome in my life. You are welcome in God's kingdom."

Journal

In theory, hospitality is a fabulous idea. In practice, things can get sticky. Running right alongside a desire to welcome and care for strangers is the God-given desire to love and protect our families and to be wise about our possessions. So how can we balance the radical call of hospitality with wisdom about what is safe or good stewardship? There's not a simple answer to this quandary.

In your journal, select one of these questions to guide your reflections on hospitality:

- What's your honest, gut-reaction to Jesus' teaching in Luke 14:12–14? Why?
- How is fear currently limiting your practice of hospitality?
- What's the difference between being wise and being fearful when it comes to hospitality?
- How do you feel most challenged to grow in reflecting God's welcome through your life?

Pray

There are many symbols of welcome in our world, but perhaps none are as poignant as the dinner table, front door, and welcome mat. Go to one of these areas in your home and touch that symbol. Kneel down by the welcome mat, sit at your table, or place your hands on your front door.

Pray about the welcoming life you desire to live. Ask God to open your eyes to the needs of those he may want you to invite into your life; invite God to grow in your heart a mind-set that reflects his welcoming love. Pray something like this:

God, you generously welcomed me home.
God, you swung your door wide open and
beckoned me inside.
God, you invite me to feast at your table of abundance.
Give me a hospitable heart like yours.
Shape my life so it warmly invites, proclaiming
your "Welcome!" to a world in need.

day 20

Loving Neighbors

Examine

In an attitude of prayerful listening, read the words of Jesus in Luke 10:25–37. Take time to let Jesus' parable sink in, then use these questions to guide in taking notes:

- What is your reaction to the explanation of what is required for eternal life (vv. 25–28)? How critical are these ideas to understanding the good news?
- Who do you most relate to in this parable? Why?
- What adjectives would you use to describe the actions of the Samaritan?
- How does Jesus' parable challenge you?

Pray

"Who is my neighbor?" the law expert asked, seeking to justify himself (Luke 10:29). Like the law expert, we want to justify ourselves—our choices, our boundaries, the limits of our love. "Who is my neighbor?" we each ask.

And Jesus' answer is anything but comforting. It will convict us to the core every time. We're not merely to love and welcome those we know, care for, and are comfortable with. In Jesus' kingdom values, even enemies become neighbors we are to love (see Matt. 5:43–47)!

True neighbor-love invites us to see the people around us through an entirely different lens. "The places and people from whom we might turn away are those to whom, in Christ, we are meant to turn," says Mark Labberton. "In the places of injustice, suffering, need and death, we are meant to look and see, love and serve. This is the new vision that comes from worshiping the One who wants our vision to reflect his."[6]

Pray through these questions: Who is hard for me to love and welcome? Whom am I tempted to pass by or turn away from? In honesty and sincerity, pray for God to help you see who your neighbors are . . . and to love them.

Worship

Author Tim Keller reminds us,

> According to the Bible, we are all like that man, dying in the road. Spiritually, we are 'dead in trespasses and sins' (Eph. 2:5). But when Jesus came into our dangerous world, he came down our road. And though we had been his enemies, he was moved with compassion by our plight (Rom. 5:10). He came to us and saved us, not merely at the risk of his life, as in the case of the Samaritan, but at the cost of his life. On the cross he paid a debt we could never have paid ourselves. Jesus is the Great Samaritan to whom the Good Samaritan points."[7]

Reflect again on Luke 10:25–37. How has Jesus shown you the essence of neighbor-love? How have you received his gracious love and been changed by it?

Worship Jesus for his generous, welcoming love. Express your true and deep gratitude for the love that turned you from God's enemy into his friend.

day 21

Loving Others Equals Loving Jesus

Ponder

Serving the needy, caring for the vulnerable, and welcoming the outcast can be really hard. What if we're met with ingratitude? What if it's a task that's gross, smelly, or repulsive? What if it has nothing to do with our talents or passions, but instead leaves us exhausted or even discouraged?

We find motivation to serve, welcome, and minister to others in our love for Jesus. "Whatever you do, work at it with all your heart, as working for the Lord. . . . It is the Lord Christ you are serving" (Col. 3:23–24). Jesus described this spiritual reality quite powerfully in his parable of the sheep and goats. Read Matthew 25:34–40.

Focusing on Jesus can provide motivation for ministry that perseveres when we're tired, discouraged, or even repulsed. "Practitioners often speak of seeing Jesus in the people in the soup line, seeing Jesus through their dirty clothes and broken spirits, seeing Jesus 'in a distressing disguise,'" writes Christine Pohl. "The sight of Jesus does not eclipse the particular human being who stands there in need, but it challenges Christians to offer the most gracious welcome possible."[8]

Love for Jesus compels us to serve, give, and welcome far beyond what our normal, self-centered instincts would require of us. How does this idea of seeing Jesus in others and serving Jesus while serving others motivate you? Convict you? Inspire you?

Create

Make a simple and beautiful picture representing the key ideas of Jesus' words in Matthew 25:31–46.

Use a white crayon to write *Jesus* in bold lettering on the bottom of a paper. Next, use watercolor to paint the entire paper in a colorful, flowing design. (The word *Jesus* should clearly appear as the crayon wax repels the paint.) When the paint dries, use a black marker to decoratively write phrases describing the needs in Matthew 25 on the top part of the paper ("I was hungry . . . I was thirsty . . . I was a stranger . . ."). In the remaining space, use red to write: "Whatever you did for one of the least of these . . . you did for me" (Matt. 25:40).

Hang up your creation somewhere in your house or workspace to remind you to find motivation to actively minister to others in your love for Jesus himself.

Pray

Mother Teresa is a famous figure to us today. But we must remember she was a regular human being, like you and me. Rather than the romantic, idealized vision of service we sometimes have, Mother Teresa's work caring for the poor, sick, and dying was tiring and difficult. It was her focus on loving Jesus that sustained her. She prayed, "Dearest Lord, may I see you today and every day in the person of your sick, and whilst nursing them, minister unto you. Though you hide yourself behind the unattractive disguise of the irritable, the exacting, the unreasonable, may I still recognize you and say, 'Jesus, my patient, how sweet it is to serve you.'"[9]

Use Mother Teresa's prayer as a springboard to write a short prayer to God, focusing on your desire to love Jesus through your love and concern for others.

days 22–30

Created to Shine

day 22

Empowered

Examine

Here is some good news about the good news from Jesus: "You will receive power when the Holy Spirit comes on you; and you will be my witnesses" (Acts 1:8).

As a believer in Jesus, the Holy Spirit lives within you and is at work, empowering you to be a witness through your words and through a transformed life!

Read these passages and take notes by writing short, personalized statements about the Spirit's work based each passage. (For example, "The Holy Spirit changes my character.")

- Luke 24:49
- John 14:26
- John 15:26–27
- John 16:13
- Acts 1:8
- Romans 8:9–17
- 1 Corinthians 12:4–7
- Galatians 5:16–26
- Ephesians 3:16

Reflect on what you've written, answering these questions: How do these passages encourage you? From reading Galatians 6:9–10, how do you understand the balance between what God empowers you to do and what you are to use your strength to do as Jesus' witness to the world? Which idea about the Holy Spirit's power do you want to more purposefully focus on and embrace in your life?

Interact

Discuss these questions with a close Christian friend: When have you experienced the Holy Spirit giving you power or strength to proclaim the good news in words or in actions? In what less "dramatic" or noticeable ways do you think the Holy Spirit is empowering you to grow, change, and share God's love? How can we encourage each other in being more aware of and relying more upon the Holy Spirit's power in our lives?

Worship

"The Holy Spirit is God's empowering presence, and what he empowers in us is a life of blessing and salvation, a life of resurrection," writes Eugene Peterson.[1] It can be very easy, amid all this discussion of what it means to live a gospel-proclaiming life, to be down on ourselves—to focus on what we're *not* doing or how we feel we're failing.

Instead, focus now on the positive, blessed, and beautiful work God has been doing in your life! In gratitude and thankfulness, express praise to God for his power that has been changing, growing, and shaping you.

Use these prompts to focus your expressions of gratitude and praise:

- What is a character flaw or sin you have struggled with that God is helping you to overcome?
- What is an area of emotional or spiritual immaturity that you have grown beyond? How are you maturing?
- What fears, worries, or anxieties are you conquering with God's help?

- How has God helped you experience joy, peace, satisfaction, or intimacy with him?
- How have you grown to know God better in recent months or years?
- How has God's presence been a blessing to you in your everyday life?
- How is God's Spirit enabling you to live a life of resurrection, newness, forgiveness, hope, contentment, and freedom?

Thank God!

day 23

Led

Ponder

One critical role the Holy Spirit plays in our lives is in leading us (Gal. 5:18, 25). At times, the Holy Spirit overtly leads us, giving us the words we need to say to someone who needs to hear and understand the good news (see Matt. 10:19–20; Mark 13:11). At other times, the Holy Spirit leads us in more subtle ways, like . . .

- drawing our attention toward people in need and helping us to empathize with their situation;
- convicting us of a sin, habit, or attitude we need to repent of and change;
- reminding us of a Scripture passage we really need at a given moment;
- leading us to feel a burden for something specific, such as a problem in our community, an area of injustice, or a nation in need;
- directing us to do something specific, such as performing an act of service or kindness, going to a certain place, or speaking to a particular person; and
- inspiring us to deepen our connection with God.

However, the Holy Spirit doesn't usually shout over the noisy chaos of life. Instead, the Spirit of God "speaks" just quietly enough that we're invited into a life of listening. We can sense the Spirit's leading as we quiet our hearts, spend time in patient waiting on God, reflect on God's Word, intentionally tune our hearts to the Spirit's presence in our lives, ask God to lead us, and faithfully to obey and respond. As we purposefully make ourselves available to God, we're able to respond to the Spirit's leadings in freedom and trust.

What factors in your life (outer circumstances, inner chaos, lifestyle, habits, etc.) may be causing you to miss the Spirit's promptings in your life? How can you tune in to the Spirit's leading in your life today?

Journal

One powerful example of the Holy Spirit's leading is recorded in Acts 8:26–40. Read the passage now.

The Spirit of God led Philip to a specific place and a specific person: a divine appointment. The Spirit of God was already at work in the Ethiopian man's life; he was drawn to God's truth and ready to hear more. The Spirit of God revealed the truth of the good news through Scripture and through Philip's words.

This is a remarkable and miraculous story! But it is a story God repeats over and over again.

Who might the Spirit be nudging *you* toward? How might God already be at work in that person's life? How could you, like Philip, respond to the Spirit's leading?

In your journal, reflect on this story from Acts, responding to these questions: How does the story of Phillip and the Ethiopian eunuch personally inspire you? How might God desire you to live out a similar story with others in your life?

Pray

Spend time praying a simple prayer for several minutes. Repeat the phrase, pausing every so often to think about what your prayer means. Listen in the quietness, enjoying God's presence.

You live in me, Holy Spirit.
Empower me today, Holy Spirit.
Lead me today, Holy Spirit.

day 24

Faith and Works, Part 1

Internalize

James is a familiar and much-debated book in the Bible. But for the early recipients of the epistle, it was a much-desired letter. They gathered to listen to it, ready for it to speak into their lives with power and truth.

Approach James as the initial recipients received it—as a letter. Take time to read it aloud in one sitting with an attitude of soul-listening, imagining the mind-set of the first hearers of this text. Don't take notes or focus on issues of debate. Don't zero in on single verses. Rather, let it speak as a whole. Simply aim to hear it—to *really* hear it.

Ponder

One powerful theme interwoven throughout the book of James is that what we believe ought to show itself in what we do and how we act:

- We're to truly listen to God's Word and respond by doing what it says (1:22–25).
- As believers in our compassionate, just, and merciful God, we're to live the good news by caring for the poor, vulnerable, and overlooked (1:27; 2:1–13).
- Living the gospel means loving our neighbors as ourselves, and that includes seemingly "unimportant" people (2:1–13).

- Belief in the gospel demonstrates itself in our actions (2:14–26).
- Our actions and demeanor reveal that we are aligned with a new way of thinking as we live by values "from above" (3:13, 17–18).
- When God leads us to do good, it's imperative that we respond (4:17).
- Materialism and injustice toward the poor are absolutely contrary to the gospel (5:1–6).
- Intimacy with God through prayer empowers a gospel-transformed life (5:13–20).

What is your response to these ideas? Why do you think this theme of faith demonstrating itself in action was so critical to the early church? How important is it today—in your church, in your life, in your world? Why?

Symbolize

Jesus himself emphasized how essential it was that his followers demonstrate their faith through their actions. Read John 15:1–10.

Jesus stressed how critical it is to live a fruit-bearing life. In John 15:10, Jesus connected intimacy with obedience. As we obey God's commands, as we respond to God's Word with action, we live a fruitful life of intimacy with God.

Take time to pot a small plant (or a seed). As you dig in the soil, water the plant, and set it in the sunlight to grow, think and pray about your life. How is God working in you to produce fruitful action and God-honoring character? What is your part in producing fruit? Do you need to focus more on Jesus' call to obedience in your life?

day 25

Faith and Works, Part 2

Journal

"I will show you my faith by my deeds" (James 2:18).

Faith—believing in the good news—is intricately connected with action. Just as faith demonstrates itself in works, works proclaim our faith to the world. Our actions, demeanor, words, character, and way of life declare a message!

Think of one to three Christians you know and admire. How is the good news proclaimed through their actions (deeds, choices, demeanor, words)? In your journal, specifically describe some of the ways their actions reveal and proclaim the good news.

Act

What can you do today to proclaim the gospel through action? Who can you serve? Is there a practical need you could meet for another person? Can you do something just? In some way, can you address poverty, racism, or a larger issue of systemic injustice? Who can you welcome? Is there a neighbor you can love by extending kindness? Is there a stranger you can love as if he or she were Jesus? Are there words of encouragement, truth, empathy, compassion, grace, or hope you can speak? Words to explain the gospel message?

Decide on one intentional and specific faith-proclaiming action you will do today that is outside of your normal routine. And do it.

Pray

In an attitude of listening, take time to pray about the message your life proclaims. Use these prompts to help you enter a time of communication with God.

God, thank you for the good news! Thank you for . . .

God, your good news has changed my life—and is changing my life. I see your work in my life in so many ways . . .

God, I desire to proclaim my faith in my life! Will you show me how I can grow?

How can my life proclaim that I am forgiven and live in your grace?

How can my life proclaim the good news of your justice? Your welcome? Your compassion? Your love for the vulnerable?

How can my life proclaim the values of your kingdom?

How can my life proclaim that you are Lord of my life?

God, help the good news to always be good news to me.

Help me to shine with the light of your love.

day 26

A Life That Shines

internalize

Write out Philippians 2:12–16 in your journal. Read it slowly, and pause to reflect on each idea in this passage:

- Obedience is a critical part of a life saved by Jesus.
- God is at work in your life, shaping your will and actions.
- Your outward demeanor helps others recognize you as a child of God.
- Your life can shine like a star, showing others the word of life!

Read this passage again, inviting God to help you understand it, embrace it, be convicted and inspired by it, and to live it.

God created you to shine, and he is at work in your life, helping you to do so.

interact

"Then you will shine among them like stars in the sky as you hold firmly to the word of life" (Phil. 2:15–16).

Who has been a shining example of Christ in your life? Whose life of obedience inspires your walk with Jesus and inspires your proclamation of the gospel? Thank that person! Take time now to write and mail a card, make a phone call, or send an e-mail to her or him and express how that person's life and example has inspired you. Share words of gratitude as well as spiritual encouragement.

Create

Author Robert Lupton says in his book *Compassion, Justice, and the Christian Life*,

> The gift most valued by the Christ is the one most valued by you. The talents you enjoy most . . . those are the very gifts needed in the work of Christ's kingdom. . . . You are invited to bring your most valuable assets—your talent, experience and connections—to create for the Christ a whole new technology of compassion. Don't reach for your billfold; it is not close enough to your heart. Don't raise your hand to volunteer for another committee. . . . Rather, look within. What invigorates you? What causes you to wake up before dawn with a new idea spinning in your mind? What fuels your imagination, even when you are fatigued? Here is where you will find your most valued treasure. Here is where you will find a gift worthy of your Lord.[2]

How is God at work, uniquely shining through you?

Create a simple paper luminary. You'll need a lunch-size paper bag, sand or rocks, scissors or hole-punch or precision craft knife, a tea light (or votive candle), and matches.

Lay the bag flat and cut a simple design, such as:

- creating one or several stars,
- using a hole punch to form concentric circles, or
- cutting out a cross, Christian symbol, or unique design.

Open the bag and fill the bottom with two inches of sand or rocks. Place a candle at the bottom and set the luminary outside. At night, light the candle and watch the light shine in the darkness, illuminating your one-of-a-kind design.

Consider how you can offer your unique gifts, desires, passions, interests, and relationships to God. How can he shine through you?

(If you made a votive candleholder on day 7, place that candle and holder in your luminary symbolizing Jesus' light shining through you!)

day 27

A Missional Life, Part 1

Ponder

Missionary: a person called to another country or people group to minister to them and share the gospel.

Read that again.

Is that correct? Well, yes . . . and no. Missionaries who work in foreign countries or in full-time ministry in this country certainly have a unique and special calling from God. But *you* are a missionary. No matter where you live or what your day-to-day job is, you are called by God to shine with the light of the gospel and to be Jesus' witness to a world in need. It's a full-time, 24/7 calling.

Read Matthew 9:36–38.

Jesus, full of compassion, saw the deep spiritual need in the people who surrounded him. Do you see the same when you look out at your community? Do you see a mission field? Jesus needed workers to harvest the ripe and plentiful field. Do you view yourself as a harvester? As a missionary?

How exciting could your life become if you saw it through a missional lens? How could a normal, hum-drum, average day be transformed by viewing it as a day to live the adventure of missions?

Pray

It's not easy to view oneself as a missionary. It's counter-intuitive to our instincts—our desire to live a safe, comfy life focused on our personal interests and plans. It requires a complete shift in mind-set. It requires absolute surrender.

Frances Havergal wrote a beautiful hymn that captures the essence of this surrender; it invites us to offer up every aspect of our lives to God for him to use. Speak (or sing) these lyrics aloud as a prayer to God:

Take my life, and let it be consecrated, Lord, to Thee.
Take my moments and my days; let them
flow in ceaseless praise.
Take my hands, and let them move at the
impulse of Thy love.
Take my feet, and let them be swift and
beautiful for Thee.

Take my voice, and let me sing always,
only, for my King.
Take my lips, and let them be filled with
messages from Thee.
Take my silver and my gold; not a mite
would I withhold.
Take my intellect, and use every
power as Thou shalt choose.

Take my will, and make it Thine;
it shall be no longer mine.
Take my heart, it is Thine own; it shall
be Thy royal throne.

Take my love, my Lord, I pour at
Thy feet its treasure store.
Take myself, and I will be ever, only,
all for Thee.[3]

Journal

In your journal, write, "I am a missionary" in big letters in the center of a page.

How does it feel to write that? Inspiring? Weighty? Uncomfortable? How well does it fit your sense of identity? Why?

Surround this statement with other "I am" statements inspired by what you've learned from God's Word in this study. For example:

- I am called to . . .
- I am saved by . . .
- I am being changed into . . .
- I am empowered to . . .
- I am reliant on God to . . .
- I am gifted in . . .

When you're done, look at the page. Embrace the truth of who God has created you to be and what God is calling you to do. Invite God to help you live a missional life.

day 28

A Missional Life, Part 2

Act

Where is your mission field? Is God calling you to a foreign land? To move to a different city or minister among a certain group of people? It's possible.

Is God calling you to minister where you are now—where you live and work? Among your family, neighbors, coworkers, and friends? To minister to strangers you meet along the path of your everyday life? Absolutely!

Go on a short walk around your neighborhood or drive a bit through your community. As you do, focus on asking God who you are being called to minister to. Who may need to hear about God's love? Who may need a friend? Who needs help with a practical need? Who is vulnerable or suffering and in need of protection and justice?

As you walk or drive, think through a typical week in your life, identifying the places you regularly go and the people you frequently interact with. Pay attention to specific people, groups, or places the Holy Spirit brings to mind for you. Pray for them, inviting God to help you see the significance of your interaction with them. How might God want to work through you to communicate his love to them?

Ponder

Perhaps the most overlooked "mission field" is the one within the four walls of your home. It's easy to focus "out there"—to people abroad or to others in your neighborhood and workplace. But raising children and being married are some of the most significant relationships for sharing and living the good news for welcome and compassion, loving as you love yourself, and offering words of forgiveness, redemption, and grace!

"Neighborly love begins in the home," says author Scot McKnight. "It is attention-grabbing to love the poor, to show compassion to AIDS sufferers, and to show mercy to victims. But it is attention-deflecting to wake up in the morning and ask, 'What does my wife or husband, my daughter or son need?' and then attend to those needs. It is easier to see love in the public square than to show love in the home."[4]

Think about your home-base relationships, whether it is with your husband, children, or extended family. How can you reenvision your home-base relationships as a primary focus for showing God's love? How can you see your regular acts of service for family members as a gospel-shining opportunity? How can you be more intentional about embodying grace, kindness, forgiveness, and compassion? How can your demeanor reflect the character of God? How can you seek God's help to be more passionate about shining the good news in your closest relationships?

Create

Using the ideas in "Act" and "Ponder" above, doodle a simple "map" of your mission field. Rather than a literal map with streets drawn to scale, make it a symbolic map of your life and relationships. Draw buildings, people, shapes, or big words to represent the places you go and the people you regularly interact with. Have fun sketching things out.

Use the image to help you visualize the reality that you are a missionary and God has planted you in a specific mission field.

day 29

God's Light, Your Story

Internalize

"For you were once darkness, but now you are light in the Lord. Live as children of light (for the fruit of the light consists in all goodness, righteousness and truth)" (Eph. 5:8–9).

Spend several minutes memorizing this passage. To aid in your memorization, write it on an index card that you can carry with you throughout the day, and revisit it several times.

Invite God to help you understand and embrace your identity as a child of the light. Courageously ask the Holy Spirit to convict you of ways you may need to more intentionally live a light-life, expressing goodness, righteousness, and truth in your actions, interactions, and thoughts.

Ponder

One common idea about evangelism is that Christians are to live such good lives that others will wonder what makes us different and will want what we have. But this mind-set can inadvertently lead us to put up a "perfect" façade to the world as if we're to seem so ideal, unblemished, and sinless that others will want Jesus. It's just plain fake! And it distorts the gospel.

Our goal isn't to show people how good *we* are; it is to reveal how good *Jesus* is. And this means inviting people into our real story. One that includes struggles and sins, faults and failings, but also the joy of redemption, forgiveness, and grace! Rather than aiming to be fake, perfect-life people, instead we live as satisfied, still-a-bit-broken sinners who proclaim Jesus' transformative grace. In other words, you can be an evangelist even if your life isn't perfect.

Should you aim to live rightly as a child of the light (Eph. 5:8–9)? Absolutely, and God is at work helping you to do so. But you most accurately proclaim the gospel when you're real with others, willing to share hurts, questions, and struggles along with assurances, victories, and joys.

What façades of perfection do you need to let go of? How might God work through your willingness to be more authentic and vulnerable with others?

Symbolize

Flip through some magazine or newspaper ads (or watch a few commercials on TV). Which ads are most effective in attracting you to their product? Which fail miserably?

Physicist, mathematician, philosopher, and devout Christian Blaise Pascal urged, "Make [Christianity] attractive, make good men wish it were true, and then show that it is."[5]

Our lives—the way we talk, act, live, interact, and love—can be profoundly persuasive to others as we communicate the essence of the gospel. We're to be the "aroma of Christ" (2 Cor. 2:15) to people; our lives give others a sense of what Jesus is like and draw them to him.

Consider these questions:

- What is it about Christianity that is most persuasive and attractive?
- What deep human needs do others have that Jesus can meet? What longings can be satisfied in Jesus?

- How can you, by the way you live, make others "wish" Christianity was true? How can you make the gospel attractive by the way you act and speak?
- How can your life not only attract others to the gospel, but show others that it is true?

day 30

Be Brilliant!

Worship

For centuries throughout church history, and still in many liturgical churches today, Christians have marked the days leading up to Christmas with the "O Antiphons," traditional prayers drawn from Scripture that highlight biblical names of God and describe humanity's need for the Messiah. (The beautiful Christmas hymn "O Come, O Come Emmanuel" is based on these traditional prayers.)

Ponder or perhaps whisper aloud this "O Antiphon" prayer to Jesus:

O Radiant Dawn,
Splendor of eternal light,
Sun of justice:
Come, shine on those who dwell in darkness
and in the shadow of death![6]

This prayer is based on Isaiah's prophesy of what Jesus will one day do for all humankind—and for you. "The people walking in darkness have seen a great light; on those living in the land of deep darkness a light has dawned" (Isa. 9:2).

Worship God now in quietness. Think of the good news, of the way Jesus has dawned as a brilliant light in your personal darkness. Build upon this prayer from church history as you worship Jesus in your words. Honor the Radiant Dawn who has illuminated your life.

(Option: Get up early one day this week to watch the sunrise and worship Jesus as the Radiant Dawn for you and all humankind.)

Journal

Take some time to flip back through your journal and reflect on all that you've written during this journey. Consider what you wrote in response to the question from day 1: "What is the good news?" In light of all you've experienced with God through this journey, how might you answer that question now? How has your perspective changed? How have you been personally challenged or inspired?

Pray

Invite Jesus to speak into your life as you conclude this spiritual journey. Read Matthew 5:14–16 with an open and listening heart.

Then simply respond in prayer:

Jesus, light of the world,
You brought me out of darkness.
Help me to live as a child of light;
Shine brilliantly through me.
Amen.

Go Deeper

Want to spend more time exploring ways you can shine the good news through your words and actions? Use these ideas.

Capture a Global Vision for Authentic Evangelism

(1 to 3 hours)

About 4,200 evangelical Christian leaders from 198 countries gathered in Cape Town, South Africa, in 2010 for the third Lausanne Conference on World Evangelization. As part of their gathering, these leaders unified to express their goals in *The Cape Town Commitment*.

The Cape Town Commitment is a powerful, inspiring, and comprehensive text expressing the essential core of what it means to proclaim the good news of Jesus to a lost world.[1] Take time to read the full document, available at http://www.lausanne.org/en/documents/ctcommitment.html. Ask God to grow your vision for your part in God's work in today's world. Consider questions like:

- How does my love for God motivate and shape my love for others?
- Do I embrace God's "mission" for my life? For the church?
- How do the various issues in the "Call to Action" section of *The Cape Town Commitment* personally challenge me? How do they grow my understanding of the needs of the global church?

Try It Out

(varies)

As you read challenges in this book to embrace justice, care for the poor, and have compassion on the vulnerable, undoubtedly specific needs came to mind. God began to prod you toward one or more areas of need in your neighborhood, church, or community. Whatever it was, don't let it be just a fleeting idea. God may be leading you toward a ministry he wants you to get involved in!

Identify a specific ministry in your community and try it out for a day. For example, take a tour of a local crisis pregnancy center or volunteer at a homeless shelter for a Saturday afternoon. Shadow someone in your church who tutors at-risk kids. Attend a workshop about human trafficking or observe a night of English-language classes offered to immigrants. Whatever you select, take this next step of research as you seek to determine how God may be calling you to shine the light of the gospel through compassionate action.

A Prayer Adventure

(2 weeks)

Commit to pray daily for the next two weeks with a simple focus:

God, give me an opportunity today to shine your light in words and action.

Often we feel the need to do big projects or have huge, planned conversations with non-Christians. But in reality, often the opportunities to shine the light of the gospel are hidden within the normal moments of our everyday lives!

Pray with this focus, looking each day for at least one specific opportunity. Each night, reflect on the specific opportunities God brought your way.

Delve into the Kingdom

(4 weeks)

Take four weeks to do a personal Bible study on the kingdom of God (called "kingdom of heaven" by Matthew). As you do, invite God to inspire you to proclaim the good news of the kingdom!

Weeks 1 and 2: Research

Use a concordance or online tool to find all the uses of the word *kingdom* in the New Testament. (There are about 150, most of which describe the kingdom of God.) Read all of the passages and take thorough notes.

Weeks 3 and 4: Reflection

Review your notes, reflect on passages that most stood out to you, and seek God's leading as it all sinks in. Memorize and meditate on a few of the passages. Ponder, pray, and journal about how God is speaking to you.

(Optional: Go even deeper by reading a book like *How God Became King* by N. T. Wright, *The King Jesus Gospel* by Scot McKnight, or *The Gospel of the Kingdom* by George Eldon Ladd.[2])

Notes

Days 1–7

1. Donald P. McNeill, Douglas A. Morrison, and Henri J. M. Nouwen, *Compassion: A Reflection on the Christian Life* (New York: Doubleday, 1982), 23–24.

2. Isaac Watts, "When I Survey the Wondrous Cross," 1707, public domain, accessed August 8, 2012, http://hymntime.com/tch/htm/w/h/e/whenisur.htm.

3. Scot McKnight, *Embracing Grace: A Gospel for All of Us* (Brewster, Mass.: Paraclete, 2005), 79–80.

4. Julie Clawson, *Everyday Justice: The Global Impact of Our Daily Choices* (Downers Grove, Ill.: InterVarsity Press, 2009), 18.

5. The idea of the kingdom of God being both "already" and simultaneously "not yet" originates with Dutch theologian Geerhardus Vos and is discussed in his book *The Teaching of Jesus Concerning the Kingdom of God and the Church* (New York: American Tract Society, 1993).

6. Isaac Watts, "Jesus Shall Reign," 1719, public domain, accessed August 8, 2012, http://hymntime.com/tch/htm/j/s/r/jsreign.htm. Note: To aid in understanding for a modern-day audience, I've changed the word *peculiar* in the last stanza to instead read "Their special."

7. "The Nicene Creed," last modified November 17, 1997, accessed August 8, 2012, http://www.creeds.net/ancient/nicene.htm.

8. Unknown Russian author, Robert G. Katsunoff, trans., "As Light, O Christ," public domain, accessed Feburary 6, 2012, http://hymntime.com/tch/htm/a/s/l/asliteoc.htm.

Days 8–14

1. Though this quotation is often attributed to St. Francis of Assisi, the actual author of this ancient Christian quotation is unknown.

2. Brennan Manning, *The Furious Longing of God* (Colorado Springs: David C. Cook, 2009), 82.

3. Christian Buckley and Ryan Dobson, *Humanitarian Jesus: Social Justice and the Cross* (Chicago: Moody Publishers, 2001), 88.

Days 15–21

1. Richard Dahlstrom, *The Colors of Hope: Becoming People of Mercy, Justice, and Love* (Grand Rapids, Mich.: Baker, 2011), 14–15.

2. Harriet Beecher Stowe, "Sojourner Truth, the Libyan Sibyl," *Atlantic Monthly*, April 1863, accessed August 3, 2012, http://www.sojournertruth.org/Library/Archive/LibyanSibyl.htm. Note: Stowe recorded Truth's words in dialect that I have changed to ease understanding for modern-day readers. Stowe records Truth as having said, "When I preaches, I has jest one text to preach from, an' I always preaches from this one. *My* text is, "When I Found Jesus."

3. Carmichael was a prolific writer and poet; you can learn more about her in her books or by reading Elisabeth Elliot, *A Chance to Die: The Life and Legacy of Amy Carmichael*, rep. ed. (Grand Rapids, Mich.: Revell, 2005).

4. Learn more about Day's conversion and faith in her autobiography *The Long Loneliness: The Autobiography of the Legendary Catholic Social Activist* (New York: Harper & Row, 1952); or Paul Elie, *The Life You Save May Be Your Own: An American Pilgrimage* (New York: Farrar, Straus and Guroux, 2003).

5. Christine D. Pohl, *Making Room: Recovering Hospitality as a Christian Tradition* (Grand Rapids, Mich.: Eerdmans, 1999), 21.

6. Mark Labberton, *The Dangerous Act of Loving Your Neighbor: Seeing Others through the Eyes of Jesus* (Downers Grove, Ill.: InterVarsity Press, 2010), 170.

7. Timothy Keller, *Generous Justice: How God's Grace Makes Us Just* (New York: Dutton, 2010), 76–77.

8. Pohl, *Making Room*, 22.

9. Calvin Miller, ed., *The Book of Jesus: A Treasury of the Greatest Stories and Writings about Christ* (New York: Simon & Schuster, 1996), 510–511.

Days 22–30

1. Eugene H. Peterson, *Practice Resurrection: A Conversation on Growing Up in Christ* (Grand Rapids, Mich.: Eerdmans, 2010), 202.

2. Robert D. Lupton, *Compassion, Justice, and the Christian Life: Rethinking Ministry to the Poor* (Ventura, Calif.: Regal, 2007), 122.

3. Francis R. Havergal, "Take My Life and Let It Be," 1874, public domain, accessed August 8, 2012, http://hymntime.com/tch/htm/t/a/k/takemyli.htm.

4. Scot McKnight, *The Jesus Creed: Loving God, Loving Others* (Brewster, Mass.: Paraclete, 2004), 55–56.

5. Blaise Pascal, *Pensées*, trans. A. J. Krailsheimer (New York: Penguin, 1995), 4.

6. The "O Antiphons" prayers are public domain; they can be found in many Christian liturgical resources. This prayer was taken from "Advent Prayers, Devotions, and Collects," accessed August 8, 2012, http://www.churchyear.net/adventprayers.html.

Go Deeper

1. "The Cape Town Commitment," The Lausanne Movement, last modified October 2011, accessed April 16, 2013, http://www.lausanne.org/en/documents/ctcommitment.html.

2. N. T. Wright, *How God Became King: The Forgotten Story of the Gospels* (New York: HarperCollins, 2012); Scot McKnight, *The King Jesus Gospel: The Original Good News Revisited* (Grand Rapids, Mich.: Zondervan, 2011); George Eldon Ladd, *The Gospel of the Kingdom: Scriptural Studies in the Kingdom of God* (Grand Rapids, Mich.: Eerdmans, 1959).